INTERIOR

Details

— ✳ —

The Designers' Style

INTERIOR

Details

——✠——

The Designers' Style

Noel Jeffrey

Architecture & Interior Design Library

An Imprint of
PBC International, Inc.

Distributor to the book trade in the United States and Canada
Rizzoli International Publications Inc.
300 Park Avenue South
New York, NY 10010

Distributor to the art trade in the United States and Canada
PBC International, Inc.
One School Street
Glen Cove, NY 11542

Distributor throughout the rest of the world
Hearst Books International
1350 Avenue of the Americas
New York, NY 10019

Library of Congress Cataloging–in–Publication Data

Jeffrey, Noel
     Interior details : the designers' style / by Noel Jeffrey.
        p. cm.—(Architecture & interior design library)
     Includes index.
     ISBN 0–86636–288–6   (Pbk ISBN 0-86636-349-1)
       1. Architecture—Details—Pictorial works. 2. Interior decoration—United
States—Pictorial works. 3. Interior decoration accessories—Pictorial works.
I. Title. II. Series: Architecture & interior design library.
NA2850.J44 1994   94-5871
728—dc20   CIP

CAVEAT– Information in this text is believed accurate, and will pose no problem for
the student or casual reader. However, the author was often constrained by information
contained in signed release forms, information that could have been in error or not includ-
ed at all. Any misinformation (or lack of information) is the result of failure in these attes-
tations. The author has done whatever is possible to insure accuracy.

Color separation, printing and binding by Toppan Printing Co. (HK) Ltd. Hong Kong

Printed in China

10 9 8 7 6 5 4 3 2 1

For Lynn and Gerard

C O N T E N T S

FOREWORD

Upon entering a comfortable and stylish room—in a private home or even in a designer showcase house—most of us have overheard (or perhaps even offered) the comment, "this room is perfect...everything works so well." All the elements of design come together in harmony in such rooms—the selection and placement of furniture, the fabrics, finishes and accessories, and the myriad elements that create a special place.

Empty spaces, however, are not transformed overnight, much less by chance or by whim. Whatever is chosen must work within the plan of the room as a whole; the resulting magic is the inspired execution of the design process by such talented individuals as Noel Jeffrey and other leading American designers.

The rooms that follow are polished and professional with clearly defined styles executed by the well-known and well-established designers of our time—and there are lessons to be learned here by both amateur and professional alike.

In INTERIOR *Details*: *The Designers' Style*, Noel gives us an intimate look at the steps involved. He begins, as all of us do, with a bare room accented with any number of architectural details such as wood floors, a fireplace, windows and paneling. He then leads us on a logical path toward the creation of a well-planned and personalized space, employing the disciplines, details and expertise that all designers utilize daily in the creative art of interior design.

—Chris Casson Madden

INTRODUCTION

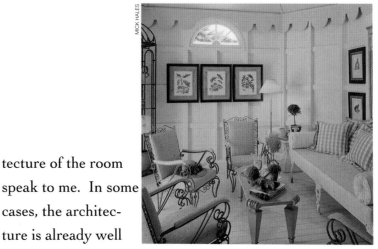

A well-designed room seems so effortless to the casual observer. In many instances, it seems as though the room has always been that way. In a traditional room, the moldings and architectural detailing anchor the room to its place in history. In a sleek, modern room, the absence of these very details allows it the freedom to look toward the future. In INTERIOR *Details: The Designers' Style,* I've attempted to show how an interior comes together by taking a look at the fundamental aspects of a room.

To begin, a room must be defined. The definition comes from the room's most basic element—its architecture. When approaching a new design challenge, I often let the archi-

tecture of the room speak to me. In some cases, the architecture is already well defined and needs only to be enhanced by the decorating of the room. In other cases, the architecture may be poorly defined and needs to be helped along by slight adjustments to improve its integrity. It's remarkable how a simple change in detailing—enlarging a crown molding, for example—can correct the overall proportions of a room and make it pleasing to the eye. In the worst case, a room may lack significant architectural details altogether, or it may possess very poor ones. In this instance, it is necessary to completely change what is

there, and then redefine the space according to the new requirements. For a designer, this is a most exciting endeavor: it's like working on a blank canvas. The major difference is that the designer's first thoughts will be questions like how will the room be used? And, how will people move through the room? It may be necessary to create a larger or smaller space. Once these basic issues are decided, the large surfaces come into play. What distinguishes the walls, the ceiling (the most forgotten element of any room), and the floor? The designer then proceeds through the actual detailing of moldings, doors, built-ins, and so forth. The definition becomes more

precise. A shell is being created for the next phase—establishing the room.

It is in this phase that the interior begins to reflect individual taste. Color sets the mood, while other elements provide movement. I've always felt that the placement of furniture connects it to the architecture of the space. Furniture also determines how one will move through the space. Fabrics provide softness and texture, making the room more human in quality. Window treatments often provide a very strong sense of personality. They can make a room feel cozy and warm. Or, in the absence of window treatments, for example, the feeling can be cool. Lighting plays a very interesting role in the establishment of the room. It can change the personality of the interior depending upon how it is used. It differs greatly from the other elements in that it is never static—it continually changes, depending upon the time of day. Even though these major elements have been established, and the interior has been architecturally defined, it is not complete until it passes through the next phase.

No matter how perfect a room is architecturally, and no matter how well the furniture has been planned, the space doesn't come to life until it is filled with beautiful objects, flowers and art. There is, obviously, no rule of thumb as to how much and what kind. It is essential to fill a space with things that reflect the personality of the occupant. Collectibles and accessories, mirrors and artwork play a very similar role to lighting. They enhance and can easily change the mood of the room.

As INTERIOR *Details: The Designers' Style* reveals in the pages ahead, a successful interior is the result of many different aspects coming together in balance and harmony.

—Noel Jeffrey

Defining
THE
ROOM

✠

The interior design of every room
begins with a look at the elements
that enclose the space. The height
of the ceiling, the width of the windows, and the layout of the space
are the elemental building blocks
that set the parameters for an interior design scheme. A room with
outstanding architectural details, or
good "basic bones," might make the
perfect backdrop for a minimal
arrangement of furnishings. On the
other hand, such added elements as
streamlined built-ins or a decorative
wall molding can enhance a lacklus-
ter space.

This section focuses on the main
elements that define the parameters
of a room. The projects reviewed
highlight how each designer has
built upon the foundation created
by the textures, colors, materials,
and proportions inherent in the
planes that carve out space.

Walls

— ✠ —

Walls create the boundaries that establish and define the parameters of a room.
They serve as a backdrop for the mix of furniture, finishes, accessories, and surfaces brought together in a space. Often, walls serve as a canvas upon which a
color palette is established; sometimes a wall of windows or mirrors expands the
sightlines of a room.

Walls can be created from or finished with almost any material: stone, steel, fabric,
wood, brick, glass, plaster, or tile. What these disparate types have in common is
their function as a visual boundary or enclosure for furnishings.

Many walls in apartments and houses are finished with plaster or plasterboard,
with paint treatments establishing a period look or design theme. Faux marbre,
stippling, and numerous other techniques enhance the flat surface. For a more textured look, other methods and materials—such as stone, marble, and moldings—
provide depth. Chosen well, the right wall surfaces can set the stage for an interior
design and cue the selection of everything set within their boundaries.

Exposed brick provides color and texture in this rustic room by Victoria Hagan Interiors.

RIGHT:

Juan Montoya added a raised grid of rectangular panels to the plain walls of this entry hall. The monochromatic wall provides a textured backdrop for treasured artwork and furnishings.

BELOW:

Plain plaster walls painted a light shade of cream make this dining room appear more expansive. Mariette Himes Gomez painted moldings and dado a stark white to emphasize the architectural details.

ABOVE:

By applying a grid of molding to a plain wall, architect Lee Mindel of Shelton Mindel creates a textural backdrop in this living room.

RIGHT:

Architect Lee Mindel of Shelton Mindel covers a curved wall with a grid of wood molding in this entry hall. The wall grid reiterates the pattern of slate squares set into a wood floor.

Exposed wood beams and raw wall boards were painted white to soften the lines of this dining pavilion designed by architect Lee Mindel of Shelton Mindel.

19

RIGHT:

A trompe l'oeil border of garlands, tassels, medallions, and ribbons adds interest to this room designed by Noel Jeffrey. The faux marbre crown molding tailors the ceiling line.

LEFT:

Noel Jeffrey selected a faux bois treatment, based on a pattern originally designed by Jean Michel Frank, to heighten depth and detailing in this room. The stylized pattern is echoed by upholstery fabrics.

OPPOSITE:

Highly glazed, burgundy walls set off a large colorful portrait by Botero in this dining room designed by Noel Jeffrey. Faux marbre molding adds to the ambience.

Noel Jeffrey arranges a group of etchings depicting Classical themes around an antique table and lamp in this sitting area. The muted tones of the artworks complement the honey-colored faux bois surface of the walls.

Billy W. Francis arranges objets and art against the subtle backdrop of a raised paneled wall in this setting.

Charlotte Moss uses a field of pale roses above a dark chair rail to soften the lines of this traditional living room.

OPPOSITE:
The two-toned checkerboard pattern of this wallcovering unifies a bedroom and hall area designed by James Egan. The muted yellow tones work well with painted molding and trim.

Floor-to-ceiling fabric panels hung along the walls of this living room camouflage windows and doors. The pale backdrop sets off a collection of classic modern furnishings arranged by Stephen Mallory.

RIGHT:

Geometric wood panels are placed in an alternating pattern to create visual interest in this bedroom. Ronald Bricke kept most surfaces white for a unified, serene scheme.

BELOW:

Noel Jeffrey upholstered a wall in a grid pattern to create architectural interest in this bedroom. Buttons tufted into intersecting corners underscore the tailored look.

Sheer white draperies hung along a purple wall are a serene backdrop in a bedroom by Ronald Bricke. An adjacent mirrored wall visually expands the space.

DANIEL EIFERT

WILLIAM WALDRON

ABOVE:

Toile draperies and wallpaper evoke a French Country ambience in this dining room. For an unexpected twist, Katherine Stephens placed a still life against an antique mirror.

LEFT:

A curved tile wall inlaid with gilt mosaics in a floral pattern are a luxe look in this bathroom designed by Victoria Hagan.

29

PETER VITALE

ABOVE:

Continuity is achieved by designer Greg Jordan in this bedroom by using the same handpainted design on both walls and bed drapery.

OPPOSITE:

*A commissioned mural of stylized Classical figures
enhances the floating wall between living and dining
rooms designed by Noel Jeffrey.*

ABOVE:

Mirrored walls reflect light and views of the surrounding landscape in this airy bathroom by Michael de
Santis.

RIGHT:

Highly lacquered hunter green walls set off light-hued
fabrics and accessories in a living room designed by
Kevin McNamara.

OPPOSITE:

Mark Zeff lined the walls of this bath/dressing room
with floor-to-ceiling draperies for a soft and sensuous
scheme.

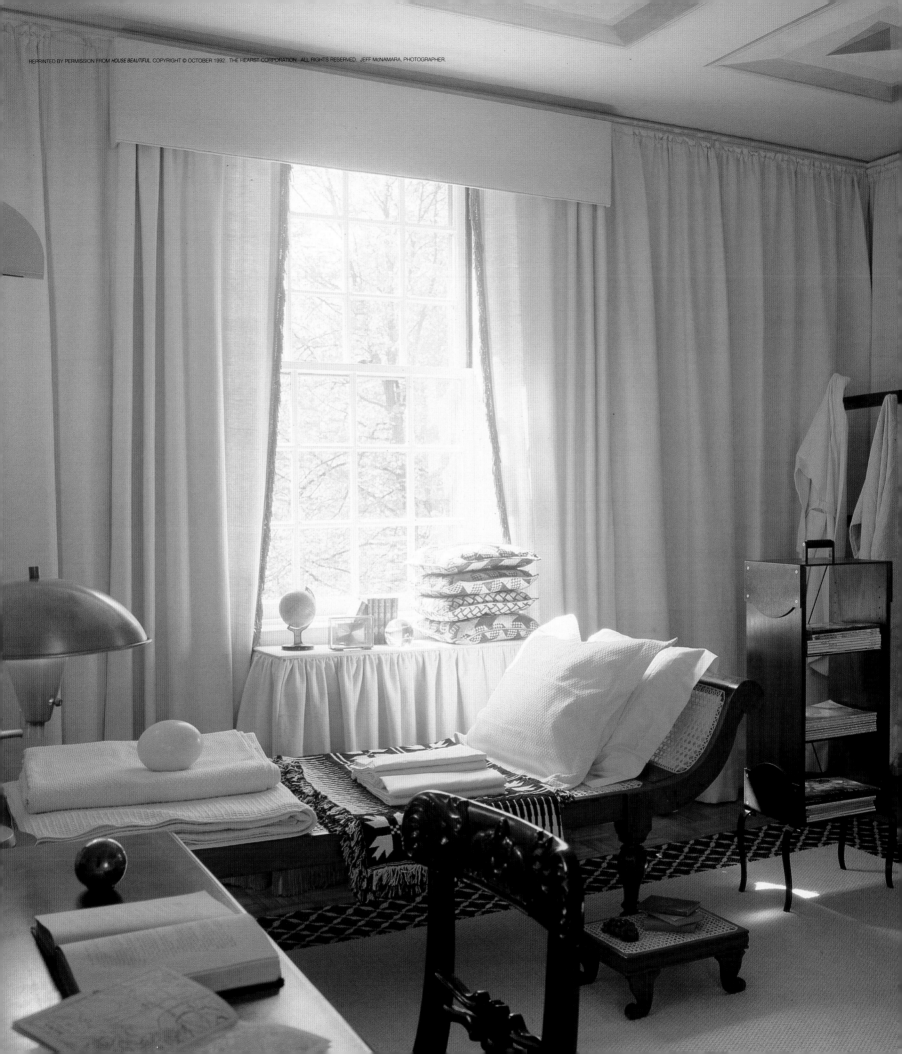

Floors

— ✠ —

What's underfoot is an important element in the creation of an interior design
scheme. Upon entering a room, a visitor first experiences the tactile sensation of
putting one foot forward after the other onto a surface: soft rug, hard marble,
creaky wood.

The flooring surface also establishes the primary horizontal plane in a room. An
expanse of gray carpeting can unify a space, while a series of Oriental rugs atop a
hardwood floor establishes distinct seating areas or walking patterns.

Hard or soft surfacing is the main question when selecting a flooring material.
After that, the options are limitless—from a cushiony carpet to firm terra-cotta
pavers. What follows is a broad range of floor treatments designed to complement
distinctive interiors.

MICK HALES

OPPOSITE:

*In an airy poolhouse designed by Noel Jeffrey, a
sponge-glazed checkerboard pattern enhances a white
wood floor.*

LEFT:

*A sun medallion and whimsical border enliven the
floor of a bathroom designed by Victoria Hagan.*

BELOW:

*Victoria Hagan sets off the sleek lines of a mostly
white bathroom with a mosaic border treatment
mixing several patterns.*

PREVIOUS PAGE:

*A faux bois stencil treatment adds a richness of
pattern to this wood floor in a foyer designed by
Noel Jeffrey.*

The ceramic tile floor in this kitchen designed by Noel Jeffrey is durable and thoroughly modern. A monochromatic palette enlarges the look of the long narrow space.

The black and white checkerboard patterned floor in this kitchen designed by Juan Montoya is a classic backdrop for pale cabinetry and sleek furnishings.

OPPOSITE:

Scott Bromley combined an expanse of slate and a similarly hued carpeted platform for continuity in this apartment.

DAN CORNISH

BILLY CUNNINGHAM

ABOVE:

The bold graphics of this rug pick up the hues of the corner banquette. Bleached wood flooring in this room by architect Lee Mindel of Shelton Mindel lets modern furnishings take center stage.

RIGHT:

Juan Montoya treats a wood floor with an exuberant painted zigzag pattern for an unexpected twist in this living room.

OPPOSITE:

Easy-to-maintain terra-cotta pavers and a sisal rug are casual elements in this sunroom designed by Ronald Bricke.

Robert Metzger uses an inlaid wood floor rather than a rug to define the dining area in this room.

A wood floor laid in a chevron pattern defines understated elegance in this room designed by Victoria Hagan.

In a room by Juan Montoya, a painted patterned floor in two muted shades is a serene anchor for furnishings.

In this room designed by Mark Zeff, parquet flooring laid in a herringbone pattern accompanies an eclectic mix of furnishings.

BELOW:

Ron Grimaldi for Rose Cummings, Inc. establishes contrast in this living room by grouping formal antique furnishings atop an aged parquet floor left bare.

ABOVE:

The Cooper Group juxtaposes metal finishes with the earthiness of distressed floor tiles.

RIGHT:

An antique Oriental carpet atop a travertine floor is the perfect accompaniment to gilt French furnishings arranged by Stephen Mallory.

A faux bois pattern enhanced by floral medallions provides a rich look for this handpainted floor designed by Gary Crain.

Ceilings

— ✠ —

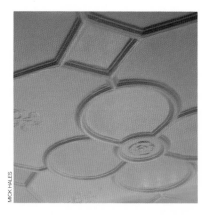

Often overlooked as an interior design element, creative ceiling treatments can transform the look and lines of a room. One doesn't have to settle for a plain white ceiling when such treatments as plaster tracery, medallions, trompe l'oeil mosaics, or even a splash of color can create an enhanced canopy.

Sometimes ceilings, if you're lucky enough to live with lofty ones, can underscore the verticality of space. If ceiling heights are more down to earth, the surface overhead can function visually as an extension of surrounding walls. Of course, ceilings don't have to remain the flat top of a boxy room. Rough-hewn beams enhance a Country Style kitchen, while gilt recessed coves sparkle above a dining table.

On the following pages the ceiling treatments are as varied as furniture styles. Each tops off a room with its individual style.

PREVIOUS PAGE:

The tracery pattern of circles, squares, garlands, and medallions creates sculptural interest on the ceiling of this room designed by Noel Jeffrey.

ABOVE:

Trompe l'oeil tile mosaics in a Greek key pattern stand out on the ceiling in this room designed by Noel Jeffrey. A chevron-patterned border adds a tailored feeling.

RIGHT:

In a room designed by Noel Jeffrey, relief plasterwork incorporates shells, garlands, and acanthus leaves for a Classic, textured effect.

OPPOSITE:

Viewed from below, this ceiling treatment designed by Noel Jeffrey is an inviting canopy. A rag-rolled "sky" is uplighted from behind a darker suspended ceiling, while a scattering of stars adds to the ambience.

JAIME ARDILES-ARCE

ABOVE:

A recessed ceiling cove outlined by the glow of uplights adds architectural interest to this New York apartment. Scott Bromley for Bromley/Calderi Architects placed pinspots along the room's perimeter for a dramatic nighttime lighting scheme.

OPPOSITE:

Bromley/Caldari Architects created a lighted cove ceiling to enhance this contemporary dining room.

LEFT:

An arbor set atop columns enhances the garden ambience of this terrace designed by Noel Jeffrey.

BELOW:

A door's etched glass and mirror pattern, created by Dennis Abbe, continues along the ceiling in this Deco-inspired dining room. Gilt lighting coves add ambience to the interior by Noel Jeffrey.

OPPOSITE:

Juan Montoya uplighted a painted skyscape in the recessed ceiling for a serene canopy in this bedroom.

Doors

— ✠ —

As the gateway to a room, a doorway provides a sense of arrival and controls the flow of movement. Doors are the shields between public and private areas, and can be imposing or inviting.

Depending on its materials of construction, a door can change the shape and function of a space. A glass-paned series of doors can serve as a window and dividing wall between two rooms. On the other hand, a frosted glass door can add privacy to an alcove or bathroom. Sometimes a door disappears altogether, as with pocket doors, to make an entrance more open and dramatic.

The doors depicted in the following photographs employ a range of materials and decorative techniques to create memorable passages into a room.

MICK HALES

In a room designed by Noel Jeffrey, Dennis Abbe created gilded and etched-glass door panels with an Art Deco flair.

BELOW:

Sandblasted panels in this painted doorframe designed by Samuel Botero create a geometric composition of color and light, while adding privacy to an alcove entrance.

ABOVE:

Square windows inset into doors are a geometric motif unifying this environment by The Cooper Group. The windows appear in different configurations for variety.

OPPOSITE:

Noel Jeffrey framed pastel paneled doors with faux marbre molding bordered by cording. The treatment works well with moiré-covered walls and painted dado.

A raised panel mahogany door is outfitted with an ornate gold knob and escutcheon in this hallway interior by Noel Jeffrey.

*Ornately carved panel doors distinguish this foyer
designed by Michael La Rocca. The arched doorways
add architectural interest.*

ABOVE:

*In this setting, designer Sandra Nunnerly reiterates
the rich wood tones of a paneled door with the
cabinetry in an adjacent bathroom. Brass hardware
is a traditional accent.*

PETER VITALE

The repeating grid of Neoclassic door panels adds a strong sense of arrival to this formal entrance hall designed by Noel Jeffrey. The door panels, all of which open, serve the additional functions of screen, wall, and window.

© 1990 RICHARD MANDELKORN

Ronald Bricke juxtaposes the warm wood tones of this traditional door with the sleek surface of a mirrored wall. An adjacent swath of drapery adds a dramatic touch to the room's corner entry.

MICHAEL L. HILL

ABOVE:

The Cooper Group creates contrast through the juxtaposition of varied materials and textures in this pivot door design. Raw silk is combined with a brass bead detail and panel. The door knob stands out as a sculptural element.

RIGHT:

The thin lines of a floor-to-ceiling pocket door provide the perfect counterpoint to the curvaceous sculptures and painting by Botero in this dining room. Designer Noel Jeffrey selected the door's kevazingo tones to complement the grain of the expansive tabletop. When pushed back, the pocket door provides a generous entryway.

JAIME ARDILES-ARCE

Built-ins

— ✠ —

Built-in furnishings and cabinetry arise from many desires: for convenience, added storage, streamlined aesthetics, or modern style. Found in the kitchen, bathroom, bedroom, and virtually every room in a house or apartment, built-ins are the workhorses of furnishings, making every square foot of space count.

Built-in units can both hide or display possessions. They range from attractive rows of books in a burled wood bookshelf to a sleek granite-topped island anchoring a kitchen. A Neoclassic armoire can hide entertainment equipment while a recessed dining room niche proudly displays pottery.

When opting for built-ins, considerations include easy accessibility to stored material, visual continuity with other surfaces in the room, and potential multi-uses for the unit. The following built-ins are a beautiful array of resourceful, space-saving design ideas.

A built-in vanity and closets incorporate mirrored panels to streamline space in this dressing room designed by Noel Jeffrey.

RIGHT:

A streamlined kitchen island designed by Scott Bromley for Bromley/Caldari Architects features a sleek stainless steel top. The rounded edges of the island and suspended cabinets work well next to a curved wall of glass blocks.

BELOW:

Sinks can be sculpture too; Ronald Bricke designed this bathroom basin to heighten the drama in a dark, small space.

OBERTO GILI

© PHILLIP H. ENNS PHOTOGRAPHY

OPPOSITE:

Noel Jeffrey designed a granite-topped island to provide a wealth of working counter space in this kitchen.

PETER VITALE

JAIME ARDILES-ARCE

ABOVE:

A generously proportioned island provides plenty of work space plus room for eat-in dining. This contemporary kitchen, designed by Scott Bromley for Bromley/Caldari Architects, also features a space frame used as a pot rack.

LEFT:

Scott Bromley for Bromley/Caldari Architects built a lighted niche to display a collection of pottery in this contemporary dining room.

Floor-to-ceiling bookcases add Neoclassic style in a study designed by Stephen Mallory. Lighted niches spotlight a collection of sculptures and vessels.

New built-in bookcases add symmetry to this wide doorway between living and dining rooms. Molding along the bookcases coordinates with details of the door frame. The interior is by Sandra Nunnerley.

OPPOSITE:

R. Brooke Ltd. framed the doorway of this living room with built-in bookcases that support a Neoclassic scheme.

MICHAEL MUNDY

Built-in wood credenzas serve multiple functions in this room by Mark Zeff. One counter acts as a bar, while shelving provides storage for the desk work area.

BELOW:

A chaise longue and a custom bookcase turn a corner of this bedroom into a cozy spot for reading. The room was designed by Samuel Botero.

BELOW:

A Neoclassic armoire serves as a discreet entertainment unit in this room designed by Noel Jeffrey. Built-in bookshelves feature the same column detail for a unified scheme.

MICK HALES

© PHILLIP H. ENNIS PHOTOGRAPHY

OPPOSITE:

A space-saving built-in with clean lines houses stereo equipment and adds storage space. The setting was designed by George Constant.

Fireplaces

— ✠ —

A fireplace and decorative mantelpiece creates a focal point against an expanse of wall; it draws the eye whether one is standing or sitting. Seating groupings of chairs and sofas seem to naturally settle in near the warmth of a hearth.

The materials used to frame a fireplace vary widely, from a modern concrete border to a highly carved plaster mantel with a tile surround. Sometimes the sheer edges of a fireplace recess are left bare for a Modernist feeling. Whatever its design, the mantelpiece is an important element that helps to reinforce a room's particular period or style.

Mantels also are perfect places to display favorite items, perhaps photographs, candlesticks, or porcelain vases. When seasons change, fireplaces may need some thoughtful reappointing with such additions as screens, flowering plants, or brass fans.

On these pages are well conceived treatments for fireplaces and mantels, from the very formal to rustic country.

PREVIOUS PAGE:

Fluting and gold medallions highlight this fireplace in a room designed by Noel Jeffrey. The painting, sculpture, and collection of Nitsuke figures warm the setting.

RIGHT:

A bountiful vase of dried hydrangeas softens the lines of the carved wood mantel in this living room by architect Lee Mindel of Shelton Mindel.

FAR RIGHT:

Neoclassic urns and sphinxes distinguish this mantel designed by Noel Jeffrey. A checkerboard fireplace surround and leaded glass cabinet doors contrast with faux bois walls.

OPPOSITE:

For a summer ambience, Noel Jeffrey shields a dormant fireplace with a fabric screen topped off with star finials.

Dentil moldings and gilt swags and garlands along a carved mantelpiece add Neoclassic style in this living room designed by Noel Jeffrey. A brass fender and antique andirons refine the look.

Noel Jeffrey selected a gilt mirror, obelisks, and a pair of sconces to enhance this carved mantelpiece. The brass andirons and fireplace screen are a classic look.

An eclectic mix of contemporary and antique furnishings is grouped around the focal point of a fireplace in this living room designed by Samuel Botero. A large portrait and hurricane lamps draw the eye toward the hearth.

The variegated colorations of this marble mantel are set off by a black, cast-iron fireplace surround. The living room was designed by Billy W. Francis.

RIGHT:

Gary Crain uses a mantel of painted molding for an understated look in a Country Style dining room.

BELOW:

Dark Art Deco urns sit atop the carved columns of this limestone mantel in a room designed by Noel Jeffrey.

BELOW:

This serene living room was designed by architect Lee Mindel of Shelton Mindel. The rough texture of a gray concrete mantel is a good contrast to white painted brick and clapboard walls.

MICHAEL L. HILL

LEFT:

A tall white mantelpiece looks crisp against the pale blue walls of a living room designed by Ronald Bricke. The fluted carvings of the mantel reiterate the stripes of the sofa and ottoman.

BELOW:

Ronald Bricke warms the decor of this Country Style keeping room with a rustic fireplace and dutch oven.

A stained wood mantelpiece is paired with a black marble surround in a living room created by Richard Ridge. Above the mantel, large sconces and a formal portrait emphasize the verticality of the lofty space.

PIETER ESTERSOHN

*Towering vines are juxtaposed with a marble mantel
in this eclectic setting designed by Vicente Wolf.*

© 1990 MICHAEL MUNDY

*A metal fireplace surround artfully contrasts with the
shapes of a sculpture and vases in a room designed by
Mark Zeff.*

OPPOSITE:

Lack of decoration is the secret of this striking fireplace designed by The Cooper Group. The minimalist approach makes the hearth a form of sculpture.

Architectural Elements

— ✠ —

To reinforce the overall effect created by the walls, floor, and ceiling of a given space, additional architectural elements are often used with great dramatic impact. An ornate plaster ceiling medallion, mahogany paneled dado, wainscoting, or elaborate dentil molding are details that can accentuate or disguise the basic lines of a space.

Some architectural elements are added to a room strictly for aesthetic considerations. Plaster pilasters topped with antique gilt capitals, for example, can visually frame a built-in bookcase. Likewise, a sculptural suspended ceiling adds interest to a foyer.

In other interiors, hard-to-replace architectural elements can be both functional and decorative. Exposed wood ceiling beams provide structural support and rustic charm, while a curved wall of glass block can define a space and work as an attractive barrier.

Whether architectural elements play supporting or central roles in an interior design scheme depends, of course, upon the other decorative devices used in a room. The following photographs portray how well-conceived architectural elements can come into play in many areas of your home.

An unusually shaped wall cutout along a staircase artfully frames a living room designed by architect Lee Mindel of Shelton Mindel.

This bright, airy living room was designed by architect Lee Mindel of Shelton Mindel. Wall moldings and a walkway bannister reiterate the geometry of the window frame grid.

Architect Lee Mindel of Shelton Mindel incised a grid pattern along the walls of this hallway to enhance architectural lines.

LEFT:

Michael La Rocca crowns this dining room with an ornate cornice that echoes the plasterwork of the mantel below.

OPPOSITE:

A black and white checkerboard border gives this octagonal dining room by Mariette Himes Gomez an unexpected twist.

Moldings, a chair rail, and dado heighten the classic look of a living room designed by James Egan.

A double-height living room, designed by Mariette Himes Gomez, relies upon structural elements to emphasize the soaring verticality of the space.

Noel Jeffrey juxtaposed faux marbre moldings and moiré-covered walls for textural interest in this living room. A glazed dado in a complementary shade carries out the theme.

ANDREW GARN

OPPOSITE:

A recessed ceiling and coved uplighting create a rotunda
effect in this foyer by designer Juan Montoya.

ABOVE:

James Egan painted walls, moldings, and chair rail
the same shade for a serene scheme in this interior.
An Ionic column becomes the Classical pedestal for a
glass tabletop.

LEFT:

A faux marbre column and plaster ceiling beam
indicate movement from foyer to living room in this
project designed by Noel Jeffrey.

OVERLEAF:

The sculptural form of a staircase designed by Noel
Jeffrey is a strong contrast to the antique furniture in
this double-height living room.

LEFT:

Noel Jeffrey uses a faux marbre molding to accompany deep red lacquered walls in this room.

LEFT:

An archway and a half-wall help to define the boundaries between a foyer and living room. Billy W. Francis also selected a planter and antique screen to visually separate the space.

OPPOSITE:

A slanted chrome half-column is an unexpected element in this antique-filled apartment designed by Juan Montoya.

Blocky capitals atop plain columns create a Modernist colonnade framing this dining room. Scott Bromley for Bromley/Caldari Architects also uses a ceiling beam to add architectural interest.

RIGHT:

A backlighted grid of sandblasted glass adds architectural interest in a foyer. Bromley/Caldari Architects designed the slanting wall as part of the interior scheme.

RIGHT:

In a kitchen created by Scott Bromley for Bromley/Caldari Architects, chrome-clad columns and a curved glass block wall define the space.

JAIME ARDILES-ARCE

GRANT MUDFORD

Raw timber beams, skylights, and the freestanding
walls of a bathroom enclosure distinguish this interior
by Sandra Nunnerley.

A dark-stained window frame and a built-in,
slate-topped table highlight a hallway alcove designed
by Sandra Nunnerley.

This interior by Sandra Nunnerley juxtaposes the light tones of an etching and stylized Windsor chair against the backdrop of a dark paneled stair landing.

Establishing
THE
ROOM

✠

Furniture is paramount in estab- lishing a successful interior design scheme. The arrangement of furniture should architecturally reflect how the room will be used. A collection of antique pieces can evoke a historical period; coordinated or contrasting fabrics and finishes can underscore a theme or mood. Whether minimal or cluttered, the selection and arrangement of furnishings anchors the overall design of a room.

The right lighting, mix of color, and window treatments enhance the effect of furniture placement. These main components of interior design are reviewed in this section. The rooms featured vary greatly in style, but their artful juxtapositions of furnishings capture the eye.

Furniture

—✤—

Furniture, of course, is the major player in interior design. The lines of a room's chairs, tables, credenzas, and other furniture pieces immediately signify certain periods of design and personal notions of style.

The arrangement of furniture is crucial to a successful interior scheme. A room can be filled to its edges with chairs and sofas and look just right, while a Minimalist aesthetic may call for a single chair and desk atop a clean plane of wood flooring. It's in the mix—the juxtaposition of scale, materials and finishes, textures, and colors—where great rooms are created.

A room doesn't have to adhere to one historical design period or style. Many of the interior design schemes that follow feature eclectic groupings of furniture that rely upon contrast for impact. Furnishings also are easily adaptable to different rooms. A weathered desk set in a Country kitchen or a bleached armoire used as a cabinet for bathroom linens find new uses for treasured pieces.

The following photographs display rooms where the furniture arrangements are well orchestrated.

KARI HAAVISTO

Victoria Hagan Interiors selected a tall tea table, modern lamp, and a tailored sofa for this living room.

BELOW:

Mark Zeff sets an antique portrait and silver bowl atop an ornately carved headboard for an intimate scheme in this bedroom.

ABOVE:

Mark Zeff places overstuffed furnishings covered in neutral fabric against the patterns of draperies and Oriental rugs for an Old-World ambience.

LEFT:

In this living room, Mark Zeff sets dark-upholstered furnishings atop sisal for a study in contrasts. A large armoire provides storage.

OPPOSITE:

An interesting play of shapes distinguishes this dining room designed by Mark Zeff. The glass-topped table and wood chairs are strikingly offset by a zebra rug.

MICHAEL MUNDY

Overstuffed sofa, chairs, and ottoman are artfully arranged in this spacious living room designed by Noel Jeffrey.

RIGHT:

For a luxurious ambience, Noel Jeffrey placed a tufted chaise longue next to a curvaceous sofa. Pale upholstery creates an airy effect.

RIGHT:

A fringed chenille throw enhances this tufted sofa in a room by Noel Jeffrey. Classic chairs and a floral and gilded screen add to the romantic mood.

The warm hues of Biedermeier furnishings anchor a serene room by Billy W. Francis.

MICK HALES

ABOVE:

A Giacometti table, nineteenth-century Russian chairs, and a Biedermeier pedestal supporting a medieval helmet are the unusual furnishings in a room by Noel Jeffrey.

BELOW:

The bright stripes of an upholstered side chair are complemented by the curving lines of an antique table in this library designed by Noel Jeffrey.

PETER VITALE

PETER VITALE

OPPOSITE:

An English Regency bed takes center stage in this bedroom designed by Noel Jeffrey. Various antique tables provide visual interest.

LEFT:

The ornate giltwork of this antique French Empire chair adds a regal air to a room designed by Noel Jeffrey. A slender table reiterates the lines of the chair back.

Juan Montoya grouped an unexpected mix of furnishings in a corner of this bedroom. The dark Chinese screen is a colorful foil to an antique desk.

Vicente Wolf juxtaposes furnishings with varying scales and textures for a striking vignette in this living room.

OPPOSITE:

James Egan uses an antique mirrored screen as a backdrop for this living room. The finish of the French side chair echoes the feeling of antiquity.

ABOVE:

*Monochromatic sofas and chairs create several seat-
ing groupings in this Art Deco-inspired living room
designed by Noel Jeffrey.*

RIGHT:

*In a living room by Samuel Botero, contemporary
furnishings are set against a monochromatic
backdrop. The shiny bar in the corner becomes a
column-like focal point.*

ABOVE:

The carved swan detail of this antique daybed, along with the ruffled folds of a canopy, set a romantic mood in this room designed by Sandra Nunnerley.

OPPOSITE:

An abundance of furnishings and accessories warms a room designed by Charlotte Moss. Letters and other mementos surround a treasured writing desk and comfortable chair.

ABOVE:

Sandra Nunnerley bedecks a child's crib with a flowing canopy, and upholsters a comfortable club chair with a cheerful floral print.

LEFT:

Taupe upholstery on a tuxedo sofa and side chair creates continuity in this room designed by Noel Jeffrey. An Empire-influenced armoire adds style while doubling as an entertainment unit.

Lighting

—✠—

Even the best designed room is not complete if inadequately lighted. Lighting is often the hardest design variable to control, and depends on such factors as available daylight from windows or skylights, the reflectivity and glare potential of furnishings and surfaces, and a room's specific function. A busy task-oriented area such as a kitchen requires good overall direct lighting while a dramatic foyer may call for the subtle wash of coved uplights spotlighting a ceiling mural.

A well-conceived lighting plan also allows for light variances throughout the day and from season to season. Fixtures can create moods ranging from the warming glow of a book-lined study to the striking vignette of desktop objects accentuated by a halogen lamp. Indirect, direct, and ambient sources work together to create versatile lighting schemes. Fluorescent, incandescent, and halogen fixtures each provide unique properties relating to intensity, color rendering, and energy-conservation.

The decorative and functional lighting options featured in these photographs include a Chinese porcelain lamp, sculptural torcheres, an alabaster pendant, and uplights set behind plants and a shoji screen. A candle-filled setting graces one room, while natural daylight is the only source shown in another view. Illumination is limited only by the imagination.

MICK HALES

PREVIOUS PAGE:

A backlighted shoji screen creates a graphic element in this dining room designed by Juan Montoya. Uplighting in a round ceiling cove provides the perfect canopy.

RIGHT:

The pinecone motif of an Art Deco chandelier warms the decor of this entry hall designed by Noel Jeffrey.

OPPOSITE:

Hung by rust-colored cords, a pendant alabaster fixture softens a bedroom by James Egan with a luminous glow.

OPPOSITE:

Victoria Hagan Interiors enhances the still life atop this writing desk with a streamlined halogen lamp featuring a green shade.

RIGHT:

A grand candelabra is an elegant touch in this setting designed by architect Lee Mindel of Shelton Mindel.

LEFT:

Victoria Hagan Interiors brightens the eclectic mix of objects on this desktop with an adjustable halogen lamp.

JAIME ARDILES-ARCE

A contemporary fixture forms a ladder of light and shadow near artwork. The room was designed by Scott Bromley for Bromley/Caldari Architects.

LEFT:

Scott Bromley for Bromley/Caldari Architects emphasized the contemporary ambience of this dining room with a modern "chandelier" of exposed bulbs, cords, and frame.

BELOW:

A pair of candlestick lamps adds formal symmetry to a room designed by Michael La Rocca.

LEFT:

Sconces set behind lush plants cast dramatic shadows along the walls of this New York apartment by Scott Bromley for Bromley/Caldari Architects.

BELOW:

Recessed fixtures create grids of light along a wall and hallway ceiling in this installation by Scott Bromley for Bromley/Caldari Architects.

RIGHT:

In the entryway, spots recessed into the wall light one's path while contemporary fixtures overhead add architectural interest. The interior scheme is by Bromley/Caldari Architects.

OPPOSITE:

A zigzag of neon snakes through the dining area in this apartment by Bromley/Caldari Architects. Track fixtures spotlight art in the hallway, while recessed spots provide task lighting in the kitchen.

BELOW:

Stylish sculptural desk lamps and a wall sconce set into a black column work well in this Modernist-influenced bedroom by Ronald Bricke.

ABOVE:

A variety of lighting fixtures work together to create a dramatic landscape in this apartment. Bromley/Caldari Architects selected sconces, wall-washers, recessed spots, and neon to highlight the urbane scheme.

Curved sconces reiterate the lines of round-edged chairs and tables in this setting by Ronald Bricke. The uplighting casts a subtle glow.

Natural daylight flooding from a window enlivens a still life arranged by Albert Hadley of Parish-Hadley.

In a foyer and hallway designed by Robert Metzger, sconces and overhead fixtures illuminate artwork and softly hued walls.

A Classical urn serves as the base of a bedside lamp in this interior by Billy W. Francis, casting light on a sculptural mask.

Color

As in fashion, painting, and other visually oriented arts, interior design relies in large part upon color to create a mood or ambience. Whether integral to natural materials or applied to a room's surfaces, colors and their juxtaposition can shape and influence an overall design scheme. Cherry paneling or terra-cotta pavers create planes that warm a space. Meanwhile, billowing folds of white bed linens and draperies capture sunlight and evoke an airy quality.

Coordination and contrast are important considerations when plotting color schemes. An unorthodox combination of jewel tones for wall paint, or a mix of striped and plaid fabrics in complementary shades can lend a unique—and personal—character to a room. Then again, the uniformity of a monochromatic scheme can be a striking sea of calm.

When exploring various decorative styles, note that certain colors, surfacing materials, and their applications can be used to replicate or evoke historical periods. And while long-held ideas about colors suitable to a certain period are often observed, there is always room for improvisation.

The following photographs display colorful rooms that give a fresh perspective to residential interiors.

PREVIOUS PAGE:

Warm, jewel-toned upholstery fabrics are paired with pale pink walls in this living room by Ronald Bricke.

ABOVE:

Pale upholstery fabrics and painted walls were combined in this room by Samuel Botero. Yellow Chinese lamps are bright accents.

LEFT:

Samuel Botero covered walls with an expanse of bright moiré to complement the vibrant hues of a Cubist painting.

OPPOSITE:

Dark wine-colored walls in this room designed by Samuel Botero serve as a backdrop for black-and-white photography.

ABOVE:

Two-toned faux marbre wallcovering, set in a diagonal check pattern, is an inviting backdrop in this dining room by Sandra Nunnerley.

LEFT:

In this living room designed by Samuel Botero, fabrics and walls in shades of creamy yellow help to unify the scheme.

ABOVE:

A crisp room of white furnishings is enhanced by a spray of greenery in this serene room by Juan Montoya.

BELOW:

Wine and green fabrics reiterate the shades of the carpet in this room designed by Mark Zeff.

RIGHT:

Mark Zeff selected a bright mustard upholstery fabric to make a chair stand out in this setting. A similarly hued modern coffee table and a collection of art glass are other bright additions.

OPPOSITE:

Richly hued rugs lead the way to a Buddha set atop a purple pedestal in this hallway scheme by Samuel Botero.

LEFT:

A palette of saturated primary colors is a sophisticated scheme in this living room by architect Lee Mindel of Shelton Mindel.

ABOVE:

In a dining room, Mario Buatta sets a colorful paisley tablecloth against jewel-toned blue walls.

LEFT:

Mark Zeff selected neutral draperies and flooring to surround the bed in this room. The vibrant red fabrics atop the bed are a welcome splash of color.

OPPOSITE:

The rich wood tones of antique furnishings stand out against gray-green walls in a foyer designed by Samuel Botero.

BILLY CUNNINGHAM

MICHAEL L. HILL

LEFT:

Bennett & Judie Weinstock Interiors aligns a collection of bright boxes and animal figurines atop a dark wood table. The mustard-hued moiré wallcovering complements a Chinese lamp.

LEFT:

Deep blue walls contrast with the rich tones of wood furnishings in this dining room designed by Ronald Bricke.

RIGHT:

A patterned blue wallcovering in this room works well as a backdrop for a collection of antique perfume bottles in a space designed by Noel Jeffrey.

MICK HALES

Window Treatments

— ✠ —

Set into the walls of a room, windows naturally capture one's eye. They serve as the apertures that penetrate vertical planes, letting in natural light and opening up a space. Sometimes windows frame spectacular views. Conversely, an unattractive vista may need some creative camouflaging.

Various treatments are orchestrated to either emphasize or de-emphasize windows. Formal draperies can connote a certain period or style, while matchstick blinds lend a casual air. Other options include Roman shades, vertical blinds, swags and jabots, sometimes even decorative screens or a natural curtain of plants.

Several of the following projects left expanses of glass windows bare, emphasizing architectural detailing as well as the surrounding landscapes. How windows are treated can alter the look and mood of a room.

PREVIOUS PAGE:

Austrian shades add a Classical air to this room by George Constant.

RIGHT:

For a luxurious ambience in this bedroom, Noel Jeffrey designed the voluminous draperies to graze the floor. Ruffled and fringed valences complete the look. Lace balloon shades filter sunlight.

ABOVE:

A valence and billowing draperies of moiré silk soften the look of the windows in this apartment by Mark Zeff.

OPPOSITE:

In a room by Victoria Hagan Interiors, a gray-painted window frame set in a dormer is left uncovered for a sense of geometry.

BELOW:

Architect Lee Mindel of Shelton Mindel selected pleated shades and rectangular cornices to underscore the geometric lines of this living room.

© DAN CORNISH

MICHAEL MUNDY

LIZZIE HIMMEL

ABOVE:

A quilted treatment adds texture to monochromatic draperies and a pelmet designed by Mariette Himes Gomez.

LEFT:

Natural-finished wood shutters in a lattice-work pattern define stylish simplicity in this room by Stephen Sills.

© DAN CORNISH

A double-height expanse of uncovered glass brings the surrounding woodlands inside this house designed by architect Lee Mindel of Shelton Mindel.

Above a bar, Gary Crain left this expanse of windows bare to showcase backyard garden views.

© PHILLIP H. ENNIS PHOTOGRAPHY

Noel Jeffrey placed floral-patterned furnishings on the diagonal near expansive windows for an outdoor ambience. Windows left bare visually bring the surrounding greenery inside.

To emphasize outdoor views, an expansive arched window and flanking glass doors are left bare. In this dining room by Noel Jeffrey, woodwork is also left unstained for a natural look.

MICK HALES

OPPOSITE:

In this room designed by Noel Jeffrey, flowing draperies in a celadon green are trimmed with the same toile fabric that covers the sofa.

RIGHT:

Vicente Wolf edges linen draperies with velvet for a dramatic look in this room. A white Roman shade completes the scheme.

Light-finished wood shutters easily control light and provide a neutral backdrop in this room designed by Stephen Sills.

Fringed swags hanging from a gilt rod frame a window alcove in this room by Noel Jeffrey. Half-shades and additional swags upon the windows add to the sumptuous feeling.

RIGHT:

Gary Crain used a curved drapery rod with ram's head finials to emphasize the lines of this library's expansive windows.

BELOW:

Samuel Botero combines swagged draperies and rosettes, along with pale silk Roman shades in a neutral palette for this bay window.

MICK HALES

OPPOSITE:

Noel Jeffrey designed this window treatment to frame spectacular views of Central Park. Swags, tasseled cords, and a rich drapery fabric create an opulent ambience.

RIGHT:

In this gentleman's study, Katherine Stephens designed asymmetrically gathered draperies in a jewel-tone windowpane plaid fabric.

DANIEL EIFERT

RIGHT:

Juan Montoya covered the unusually narrow windows of this dining area with matchstick blinds that echo the finishes of the furniture.

BILLY CUNNINGHAM

JAIME ARDILES-ARCE

Dark pleated shades in this apartment by Scott Bromley for Bromley/Caldari Architects reiterate the geometry of the room's many built-in furnishings.

The Cooper Group selected expansive shades for a streamlined look in this living room. The pleated shades pull up rather than down for an unexpected framing of the window.

Moiré jabots are edged with light-hued tassel fringe in this room by George Constant. Swags are draped over the curtain rods for a cascading effect.

LEFT:

The folds of soft-pleated Roman shades are a good foil for dark woodwork in this setting for dining by Samuel Botero.

ABOVE:

White cafe curtains emphasize the lines of an arched window in this dining room designed by Katherine Stephens.

ABOVE:

Ronald Bricke selected pleated shades that diffuse sunshine in this seaside setting.

Finishing
THE
ROOM

✠

Accessories and artwork are like beautiful jewelry. They are the finishing touches in a well-designed room. Displayed collections and objets d'art are the "personal effects" that add a signature style to a design scheme. A collection of antique silver boxes will shine atop the rich wood grain of an antique table, while a grouping of black-and-white travel photographs of the desert will evoke a sense of adventure. Or a gilt-framed mirror can reflect the romantic glow of candlelight in a Neoclassical dining room.

The interiors shown in this section illustrate each designer's eye for detail—the perfect accessories and finishing accompaniments to round out and refine an interior scheme.

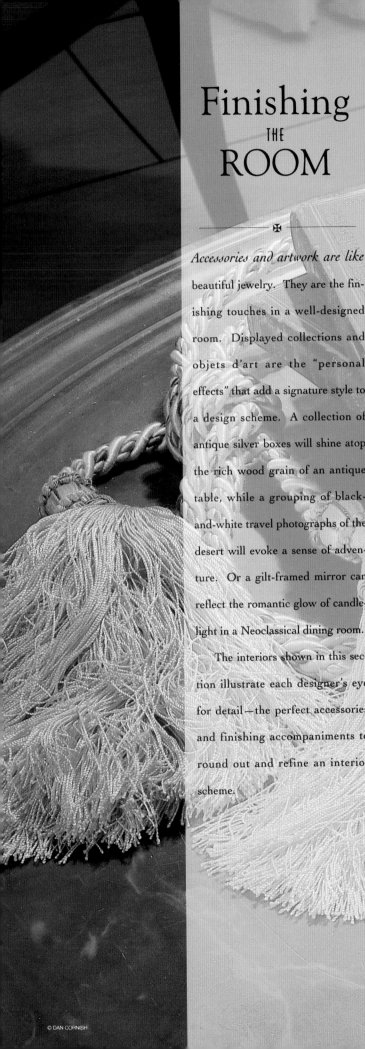

Mirrors

— ✠ —

Mirrors are a classic tool to solve a variety of interior design problems. They can visually expand space, camouflage walls, reflect other views, and increase a room's play of light.

Whether framed or covering large expanses of a wall, mirrors add to the overall style of a room. An antique gilt-framed mirror over a mantel calls forth an opulent ambience. On the other hand, an expanse of mirrored wall juxtaposed with contemporary furnishings is the essence of clean-lined modernity.

Gaze into the looking glasses in these rooms and discover a range of design solutions that put mirrors to good use.

MICK HALES

PREVIOUS PAGE:
For a romantic motif, Noel Jeffrey sets an antique mirror against the faux treatment of the walls in this vestibule.

MICK HALES

LEFT:
An intricately detailed mirror set against a red lacquered wall expands the space of this foyer designed by Noel Jeffrey.

OPPOSITE:
The patina of a Venetian mirror frame is set against the backdrop of pale walls in this serene living room designed by Noel Jeffrey.

WILLIAM WALDRON

A modern chrome-framed mirror adds strong architectural interest to this bathroom. Victoria Hagan selected a pair of vases containing white blossoms as a soft counterpoint.

OPPOSITE:

Flanking sconces reinforce the metalwork lines of this mirror in a dining pavilion designed by architect Lee Mindel of Shelton Mindel.

OBERTO GILI

MICHAEL MUNDY

ABOVE:

Stephen Sills emphasizes the generous ceiling height of this living room with a towering gilt mirror atop a low mantel.

ABOVE:

The black and gold frame of a classic dressing table mirror works well with black-matted portraits in a bedroom by Charlotte Moss.

MICK HALES

An ornate Chippendale mirror is a stunning focal point atop a sideboard in this dining room designed by Noel Jeffrey.

Pairing an antique desk with a similarly detailed mirror, designer Noel Jeffrey adds a French accent to this bedroom.

A still life of objets set against an antique gilt mirror with a Greek key pattern balances the melange of furnishings in this room by Stephen Mallory.

KARI HAAVISTO

MICK HALES

Accessories & Collectibles

—✠—

*Nothing refines the look of a room more than a carefully selected array of acces-*sories and collectibles. The objects we choose to surround ourselves with convey a strong sense of personal interest and style. From a grouping of antique timepieces resting on a library table to a mantel laden with earthenware, favorite objects evoke memories of travel and discovery. A mismatched set of teacups that caught your eye at an estate sale, or the shells you found along a deserted beach, can enhance the style of your rooms.

Theme, scale, color, and texture are important considerations in the arrangement of collectibles. Similar objects can be grouped in abundance, such as white crockery filling a corner cupboard. Or sometimes less is more, with a few colorful coffee cups set atop an antique chest.

Collections need not sit as museum pieces within a vitrine or upon an unreachable shelf. Some of the following interior design projects put collectibles to work. In one room an antique vase filled with pens and pencils personalizes a desk. The more our favorite things seem at home within our interior settings, the more our rooms come alive.

ROB MUIR

PREVIOUS PAGE:

The theme of Classical architecture and sculpture is skillfully explored in this setting by Billy W. Francis. The interplay of scale and shape, from towering obelisks to Neoclassic lamp and bust, works well against a backdrop of white plaster walls.

BELOW:

Vicente Wolf tucks old sepia-toned photos into the ribbons of folding screens for interest in this room. An artfully arranged tabletop vignette incorporates bowls of fruit, candlesticks, and framed photographs.

LEFT:

Intricately detailed silver objets accompany an architectural etching and a Classical plaster bust on this setting by Lee Mindel of Shelton Mindel.

OPPOSITE:

The color, scale, and texture of objects grouped together by Vicente Wolf form a memorable still life.

The classic contrast of black and white is explored by James Egan in this tablescape. A variety of shapes and textures, from the rough chunk of crystal to the slender iron candelabra, add visual interest.

MICK HALES

MICK HALES

ABOVE:

Noel Jeffrey set antique Chinese porcelains atop a cabinet inlaid with marquetry in this dining room.

LEFT:

A collection of Nitsuke figures adorns the mantelpiece in a living room designed by Noel Jeffrey.

JOE STANDART

ABOVE:

Floral china vases brimming with pens and roses sit near crystal and silver inkwells for this inviting scheme for a writing desk designed by Charlotte Moss.

RIGHT:

A collection of ancient vessels, arranged by designer Billy W. Francis, is dramatically set along a lacquered table. The mix of shapes, texture and scale plays well against the straight lines of a contemporary painting.

HICKEY ROBERTSON

Unusually framed mirrors with intricate wood and silver detailing create a striking play of curves in this room designed by Noel Jeffrey.

Noel Jeffrey sets a mahogany butler's table with glazed birds, a silver teapot, crystal decanters, and an abundant group of roses in an earthenware vase.

Noel Jeffrey employs a grouping of colorful postmodern coffee cups to add a whimsical touch to this traditional chest of drawers and mirror.

Architect Lee Mindel of Shelton Mindel sets off a collection of beautiful clocks with the image of a clock face discovered in an antique book. Drapery tassels and other weathered books add to the time-honored look.

Artwork

— ✠ —

Art often is the crowning touch of interior design. The luxury of collecting works of inspiring beauty is a pleasure that is well shared with guests in our homes. But artworks need not be priceless masterpieces to enhance a room; framed vintage posters, a simple line drawing, or a plaster sculpture can create an eye-catching impression.

When displaying artwork, interior designers take into account scale, color and medium. A small figurative sculpture may stand out atop a credenza, while it would be lost atop a larger table. Grouping a collection of similar photographs or etchings will make an accent wall stand out. For fine works of art, proper lighting, framing, and placement must be carefully mapped out.

As the following art-filled rooms show, almost any interior design scheme is enriched by the display of art.

A series of Matisse artwork stands out in the monochromatic corner of this study designed by Noel Jeffrey.

RIGHT:

Billy W. Francis places an antique ormolu clock below an Impressionist landscape. Two porcelain vases echo colors of the painting.

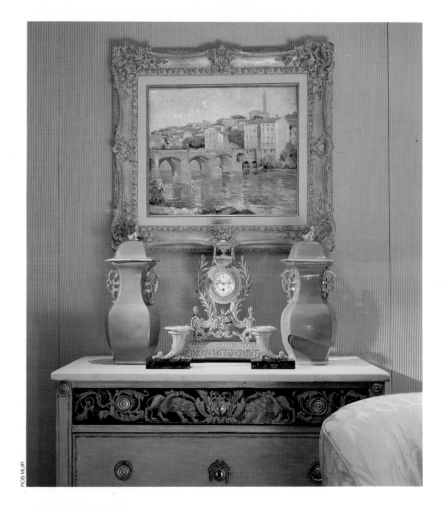

ROB MUIR

LEFT:

The Modern lines of vintage art posters enhance the ambience in this room by Noel Jeffrey. The artworks' bold graphics stand out against creamy plaster walls.

OPPOSITE:

A stark contemporary portrait provides a strong contrast to the antique sculpture, lamps, and table in this setting by Ronald Bricke.

© PETER VITALE

The slender lines of a monochromatic fashion illustration, and an equally slender candle in an antique holder, distinguish this bathroom styled by Victoria Hagan.

ABOVE:

Victoria Hagan selects three objects with distinctive shapes to enhance an antique mantel. The still life works well with the adjacent painting.

OPPOSITE:

A gold and black frame sets off a silk screen by Matisse in this setting designed by Michael de Santis. Table accessories are kept simple to let the artwork remain the focal point.

Selected Reading

An Illustrated History of Interior Decoration: From Pompeii to Art Nouveau. *Mario Praz. New York, Thames and Hudson Inc., 1982.*

Art Deco. *Victor Arwas. New York, Harry N. Abrams, Inc., 1980.*

Authentic Decor: The Domestic Interior 1620-1920. *Peter Thornton. New York, Viking Penguin, 1984.*

Biedermeier. *Angus Wilkie. New York, Abbeville Press Inc., 1987.*

Eighteenth-Century Decoration: Design and the Domestic Interior in England. *Charles Saumarez Smith. New York, Harry N. Abrams, Inc., 1993.*

Furniture: Architects' and Designers' Originals. *Carol Soucek King, Ph.D. Glen Cove, New York, PBC International, Inc., 1994.*

Imperial Palaces of Russia. *Prince Michael of Greece. Photographs by Francesco Venturi. London, Tauris Parke Books, 1992.*

In the Neoclassic Style: Empire, Biedermeier and the Contemporary Home. *Melanie Fleischmann. Photographs by Mick Hales. New York, Thames and Hudson, Inc., 1988.*

In the Romantic Style: Creating Intimacy, Fantasy and Charm in the Contemporary. *Linda Chase and Laura Cerwinske. New York, Thames and Hudson Inc., 1990.*

Inside: Discovering London's Period Interiors. *Joe Friedman. Oxford, England, Phaidon Press Limited, 1988.*

Jean-Michel Frank. Adolphe Chanaux. Text by Leopold Diego Sanchez. *Photographs by Jacques Boulay. Paris, France, Éditions du Regard, 1980.*

Manor Houses and Castles of Sweden: A Voyage Through Five Centuries. *Maita di Niscemi. Photographs by Nicolas Sapieha and Francesco Venturi. New York, Harper & Row Publishers, Inc., 1988.*

Neoclassicism in the North: Swedish Furniture and Interiors 1770-1850. *Haken Groth. New York, Rizzoli International Publications, Inc., 1990.*

New York Style. *Suzanne Slesin. New York, Clarkson Potter, 1992.*

Nineteenth-Century Decoration: The Art of the Interior. *Charlotte Gere. New York, Harry N. Abrams, Inc., 1989.*

Nineteenth-Century Interiors: An Album of Watercolors. *Charlotte Gere, New York, Thames and Hudson Inc., 1992.*

Period Details: A Sourcebook for House Restoration. *Marvin and Judith Miller. New York, Crown Publishers, Inc., 1987.*

Rooms With a View: Two Decades of Outstanding American Interior Design from the Kips Bay Decorator Show Houses. *Chris Casson Madden. Glen Cove, New York, PBC International, 1992.*

Russian Furniture: The Golden Age 1780-1840. *Antoine Cheneviere. New York, The Vendome Press, 1988.*

Russian Houses. *Elizabeth Gaynor and Kari Haavisto. Essays by Darra Goldstein. New York, Stewart, Tabori & Chang, Inc., 1991.*

Russian Imperial Style. *Laura Cerwinske. New York, Prentice-Hall Press, 1990.*

Scandinavian Painted Decor. *Jocasta Innes. New York, Rizzoli International Publications, Inc., 1990.*

The English Country House: A Grand Tour. *Gervase Jackson-Stops and James Pipkin. A New York Graphic Society Book. Boston, Little, Brown and Company, 1985.*

The English Country House: A Tapestry of Ages. *Fred J. Maroon. Charlottesville, Virginia, Thomasson-Grant, 1987.*

Victorian and Edwardian Decor: From the Gothic Revival to Art Nouveau. *Jeremy Cooper. New York, Abbeville Press, 1987.*

Appendix

Design Firms

Bennett & Judie Weinstock
    Interiors
    2026 Delancy Place
    Philadelphia, PA 19103
    215-735-2026

Bromley/Calderi Architects
    242 West 27th Street
    New York, NY 10022
    212-620-4250

Charlotte Moss & Co.
    165 East 71st Street
    New York, NY 10021
    212-772-6244

The Cooper Group
    359 Boylston Street
    Boston, MA 02116
    617-266-2288

James Egan
    c/o Noel Jeffrey Inc.
    215 East 58th Street
    New York, NY 10017
    212-935-7775

Billy W. Francis
    964 Third Avenue
    New York, NY 10021
    212-980-4151

Gary Crain Associates
    234 East 58th Street
    New York, NY 10022
    212-223-2050

George Constant, Inc.
    425 East 63rd Street
    New York, NY 10021
    212-751-1907

Gomez Associates
    506-504 East 74th Street
    New York, NY 10021
    212-288-6856

Greg Jordan
    27 East 63rd Street, #1BC
    New York, NY 10021
    212-421-1474

Juan Montoya Design Corp.
    80 Eighth Avenue
    New York, NY 10011
    212-242-3622

Katherine Stephens Associates
    200 East 61st Street
    New York, NY 10020
    212-593-1109

Kevin McNamara Inc.
    541 East 72nd Street
    New York, NY 10021
    212-861-0808

Michael La Rocca
    150 East 58th Street
    Suite 3510
    New York, NY 10155

Mario Buatta Inc.
    120 East 80th Street
    New York, NY 10021
    212-988-6811

Mark Zeff Design
    260 West 72nd Street
    Suite 12B
    New York, NY 10023
    212-580-7090

Michael de Santis Inc.
    110 Second Avenue
    New York, NY 10022
    212-753-8871

Noel Jeffrey Inc.
    215 East 58th Street
    New York, NY 10022
    212-935-7775

Parish-Hadley Associates
    305 East 63rd Street
    New York, NY 10021
    212-888-7979

R. Brooke, Ltd.
    177 East 70th Street
    New York, NY 10021
    212-535-0707

Richard L. Ridge Interior Design
    903 Park Avenue
    New York, NY 10021
    212-472-0608

Robert Metzger Interiors
    215 East 58th Street
    New York, NY 10022
    212-371-9800

Ronald Bricke & Associates
    333 East 69th Street
    New York, NY 10021
    212-472-9006

Rose Cummings Inc.
    232 East 59th Street
    New York, NY 10022
    212-758-0844

Samuel Botero Associates
    150 East 58th Street
    New York, NY 10155
    212-935-5155

Sandra Nunnerley, Inc.
    112 East 71st Street
    New York, NY 10021
    212-472-9341

Shelton Mindel & Associates
    216 West 18th Street
    New York, NY 10011
    212-243-3939

Stephen Mallory & Associates
    59 East 64th Street
    New York, NY 10021
    212-879-9500

Stephen Sills Associates
    204 East 90th Street
    New York, NY 10128
    212-289-8180

Vicente Wolf Associates
    333 West 39th Street
    New York, NY 10018
    212 465-0590

Victoria Hagan Interiors
    22 East 72nd Street
    New York, NY 10021
    212-472-1290

Photographers

Clara Aich
    218 East 25th Street
    New York, NY 10010
    212-686-4220

Jaime Ardiles-Arce
    730 Fifth Avenue
    New York, NY 10019
    212-333-8779

Samuel Bell
    305 East 63rd Street
    New York, NY 10021
    212-888-7979

Antoine Bootz
    133 West 22nd Street
    New York, NY 10011
    212-366-9041

Dick Busher
    7042 20th Place N.E.
    Seattle, WA 98115
    206-523-1426

Dan Cornish
    38 Evergreen Road
    New Canaan, CT 06840
    203-972-3714

Billy Cunningham
    26 Saint Mark's Place
    New York, NY 10003
    212-677-4904

Derrick & Love
    628 Broadway
    New York, NY 10018
    212-777-3113

Daniel Eifert
    26 Second Avenue
    New York, NY 10003
    212-473-2562

Pieter Eisterschn
    c/o Lachapelle
        Representation Ltd.
    420 East 54th Street
    New York, NY 10022
    212-838-3179

Jon Elliott
    329 West 85th Street
    New York, NY 10024
    212-362-0809

Phillip H. Ennis
    Phillip H. Ennis
        Photography
    98 Smith Street
    Freeport, NY 11520
    516-379-4273

Feliciano Garcia
    29 West 38th Street
    New York, NY 10018
    212-354-7683

Andrew Garn
    85 East 10th Street
    New York, NY 10003
    212-353-8434

Oberto Gili
    31 West 11th Street
    New York, NY 10011
    212-255-7293

Prashant Gupta
    220 Thompson Street, #6
    New York, NY 10012
    212-529-5535

Kari Haavisto
    25 West 15th Street
    New York, NY 10011
    212-807-6760

Mick Hales
    North Richardsville Road
    RA# 2
    Carmel, NY 10512
    914-228-0106

Michael L. Hill
    c/o Ronald Bricke &
        Associates
    333 East 69th Street
    New York, NY 10021
    212-472-9006

Lizzie Himmel
    50 West 29th Street
    New York, NY 10001
    212-683-5331

H.P. Horst
    188 East 64th Street
    New York, NY 10021
    212-751-4937

Dennis Krukowski
    329 East 92nd Street
    Suite 1D
    New York, NY 10128
    212-860-0912

Richard Mandelkorn
    309 Waltham Street
    Newton, MA 02165
    617-332-3246

Morgan McGivin
    c/o Kevin McNamara Inc.
    541 East 72nd Street
    New York, NY 10021
    212-861-0808

Keith Scott Morton Photography
    39 West 29th Street
    New York, NY 10001
    212-889-6643

Rob Muir
    6162 San Felipe Road
    Houston, TX 77057
    713-784-7420

Michael Mundy
    P.O. Box 97
    151 First Avenue
    New York, NY 10003
    212-529-7114

Mary E. Nichols
    1009 North Orlando Avenue
    Los Angeles, CA 90069
    310-275-2563

Lilo Raymond
    212 East 145th Street
    New York, NY 10003
    212-777-2865

Hickey Robertson
    1318 Sul Ross
    Houston, TX 77006
    713-522-7258

Bill Rothschild
    Architectural Photographer
    19 Judith Lane
    Wesley Hills, NY 10952
    212-752-3674

Durston Saylor
    14 East Fourth Street
    New York, NY 10011
    212-620-7122

Joe Standart
    5 West 19th Street
    New York, NY 10011
    212-924-4545

Peter Vitale
    Peter Vitale Photography
    P.O. Box 10126
    Santa Fe, NM 87504
    505-982-0835

William Waldron
    451 Broome Street
    New York, NY 10013
    212-226-0356

Index

Acknowledgments

It's hard to know where to begin to thank all of the people involved in producing INTERIOR *Details: The Designers' Style.* Even though there is one author, it takes many people to make a project like this happen.

A very special thanks to Kevin Clark, who very enthusiastically got me involved in the initial concept of INTERIOR *Details.* An equally special thanks to Susan Kapsis who took over as the editor mid-stream, making sure that we never missed a beat.

Style is everything to the interior designer and Garrett Schuh truly gave this book great style.

Many thanks to Mark Serchuck and Penny Sibal of PBC International who believed in me and supported me in this endeavor.

A personal thank you to Barbara Hawkins who is always there when I need her. Her advice and attention to detail helped me fulfill all of my responsibilities for this book.

I would also like to thank my friend Chris Madden for writing the foreword. I so much appreciate her continued support.

Last, but not least, I would like to thank all of the Designers and their photographers who submitted material for INTERIOR *Details.* It is the high degree of excellence of their work that has made this book so successful.